DATE DUE

GAYLORD   PRINTED IN U.S.A.

D1159709

Dream BIG

American Idol SUPERSTARS

Kris Allen

David Archuleta

Kelly Clarkson

David Cook

Chris Daughtry

Jennifer Hudson

Adam Lambert

Kellie Pickler

Jordin Sparks

Carrie Underwood

Elliott Yamin

American Idol Profiles Index:
Top Finalists from Seasons 1 to 7
(82 Contestants)

Insights Into American Idol

David Cook

Gail Snyder

Mason Crest Publishers

Produced by 21st Century Publishing and Communications, Inc.

MASON CREST PUBLISHERS INC.
370 Reed Road
Broomall, Pennsylvania 19008
(866) MCP-BOOK (toll free)
www.masoncrest.com

Printed in the United States of America.

First Printing

9 8 7 6 5 4 3 2 1

Library of Congress Cataloging-in-Publication Data

Snyder, Gail.
    David Cook / Gail Snyder.
        p. cm. — (Dream big : American Idol superstars)
    Includes bibliographical references (p.) and index.
    ISBN 978-1-4222-1507-4 (hardback : alk. paper)
    ISBN 978-1-4222-1598-2 (pbk. : alk. paper)
        1. Cook, David, 1982–   —Juvenile literature. 2. Singers—United States—
Biography—Juvenile literature. I. Title.
    ML3930.C545S69 2009
    782.42164092—dc22
        [B]   2009025462

Publisher's notes:
All quotations in this book come from original sources, and contain the spelling and grammatical inconsistencies of the original text.

The Web sites mentioned in this book were active at the time of publication. The publisher is not responsible for Web sites that have changed their addresses or discontinued operation since the date of publication. The publisher will review and update the Web site addresses each time the book is reprinted.

American Idol ® is a registered trademark of 19 TV Ltd. and FremantleMedia North America, Inc.

CONTENTS

American Idol TIMELINE ★

October 5, 2001

Pop Idol, a TV reality show created by Simon Fuller, debuts in the United Kingdom and becomes a smash hit.

Fall 2001

Based on the success of *Pop Idol*, and after initially rejecting the concept, FOX Network agrees to buy *American Idol*, a national talent competition and TV reality show.

Spring 2002

Auditions for *American Idol* Season 1 are held in New York City, Los Angeles, Chicago, Dallas, Miami, Atlanta, and Seattle.

January 21, 2003

American Idol Season 2 premieres without Brian Dunkleman, leaving Ryan Seacrest as the sole host.

May 21, 2003

- *American Idol* Season 2 finale airs.
- Ruben Studdard narrowly wins and Clay Aiken is the runner-up.
- Runner-up Clay Aiken goes on to become extremely successful both critically and commercially.

January 19, 2004

American Idol Season 3 premieres.

2001   **2002**   **2003**   **2004**

June 11, 2002

American Idol Season 1 premieres on FOX Network, with Simon Cowell, Paula Abdul, and Randy Jackson as the judges, and Ryan Seacrest and Brian Dunkleman as the co-hosts.

September 4, 2002

- *American Idol* Season 1 finale airs.
- Kelly Clarkson wins and Justin Guarini is the runner-up.
- Kelly Clarkson goes on to become the most successful Idol winner and a superstar in the music industry.

Fall 2002

Auditions for *American Idol* Season 2 are held in New York City, Los Angeles, Miami, Detroit, Nashville, and Austin.

January 27, 2004

William Hung's audition is aired and his humble response to Simon Cowell's scathing criticism make William the most famous American Idol non-qualifier and earn him record deals and a cult-like following.

April 21, 2004

Jennifer Hudson is voted off the show in 7th place, and goes on to win the role of Effie in *Dreamgirls*, for which she wins an Academy Award, a Golden Globe Award, and a Grammy Award.

May 26, 2004

- *American Idol* Season 3 finale airs with 65 million viewers casting their votes.
- Fantasia Barrino is crowned the winner and Diana DeGarmo is the runner-up.
- Fantasia soon becomes the first artist in the history of Billboard to debut at number one with her first single.

May 10, 2006

Chris Daughtry is voted off the show in 4th place, and soon after forms the band, Daughtry, and releases its debut album, which becomes number one on the charts, wins many awards, and finds huge commercial success.

April 26, 2006

Kellie Pickler is voted off the show in 6th place, and soon releases her debut album, which rockets to number one on the Billboard Top Country Album chart.

January 17, 2006

American Idol Season 5 premieres and for the first time airs in high definition.

May 24, 2006

- *American Idol* Season 5 finale airs.
- Taylor Hicks is the winner and Katharine McPhee the runner-up.
- Elliot Yamin, the second runner-up, goes on to release his debut album, which goes gold.

January 16, 2007

American Idol Season 6 premieres.

April 2007

The *American Idol* Songwriting Contest is announced.

January 15, 2008

American Idol Season 7 airs with a four-hour two-day premiere.

April 9, 2008

Idol Gives Back returns for its second year.

May 21, 2008

- *American Idol* Season 7 finale airs.
- David Cook wins with 54.6 million votes and David Archuleta is the runner-up with 42.9 million votes.
- Both Davids go on to tremendous post-Idol success with successful albums and singles.

2005 2006 2007 2008 2009

May 25, 2005

- *American Idol* Season 4 finale airs.
- Carrie Underwood wins and Bo Bice is the runner-up.
- Carrie goes on to become one of the most successful Idol winners, selling millions of albums and winning scores of major awards.

January 18, 2005

- *American Idol* Season 4 premieres.
- Some rules change:
  - The age limit is raised from 24 to 28.
  - The semi-final competition is separated by gender up until the 12 finalists.

April 24–25, 2007

American Idol Gives Back, a charitable campaign to raise money for underprivileged children worldwide, airs, and raises more than $70 million.

May 23, 2007

- *American Idol* Season 6 finale airs.
- Jordin Sparks wins with 74 million votes and Blake Lewis is the runner-up.
- Jordin goes on to join Kelly Clarkson and Carrie Underwood in the ranks of highly successful post-Idol recording artists.

January 13, 2009

American Idol Season 8 premieres adding Kara DioGuardi as a fourth judge.

February 14, 2009

The American Idol Experience, a theme park attraction, officially opens at Disney's Hollywood Studio in Florida.

May 20, 2009

- *American Idol* Season 8 finale airs.
- Kris Allen unexpectedly wins and Adam Lambert is the runner-up.
- Almost 100 million people voted in the season 8 finale.

David Cook puts his arm around David Archuleta as they wait for the results during the *American Idol* finale on May 21, 2008. The two men had been strong competitors throughout the season. In fact, judge Randy Jackson said that no matter what happened, both Davids were winners that night.

1

Dueling Davids

On May 21, 2008, with less than two minutes left in season seven of the hugely popular *American Idol* reality TV program, 25-year-old David Cook and 17-year-old David Archuleta stood side by side on the stage of the Nokia Theater in downtown Los Angeles. They were waiting to hear which man had been voted winner of the competition.

David Cook, a former bartender who had already played in several bands and recorded a solo album, stood with his eyes closed and one arm wrapped around the shoulders of the younger and shorter high school student who had been his closest rival for the past four months.

9

As they waited with hearts pounding for host Ryan Seacrest to announce the winner, the words of the three *American Idol* judges who had addressed them earlier that night were fresh in their minds. Paula Abdul reminded them that this was not really a finale but a beginning for both of them. Randy Jackson remarked that both Davids would be winners no matter what happened that night. British judge Simon Cowell, known for his sharp and often critical remarks, said simply, "For the first time ever I don't care who wins. You are both terrific people." The audience in the packed theater erupted in cheers when Ryan finally said,

"Ladies and gentleman, David and David, the winner by 12 million votes of *American Idol* 2008 is David . . . Cook!"

Surprised to Win

Upon hearing the news, David dropped his head, put his hand over his mouth, and wiped tears from his eyes. Clearly overcome by emotion, he immediately asked the audience to recognize the achievement of David Archuleta, whom he hugged; he then embraced his mother as well as his younger brother Andrew who had also tried out for *Idol* but did not make it on the show. After taking a moment to regain his composure, David said, "I started this season, much to Simon's chagrin, as a word nerd and I'm absolutely at a loss for words. Thank you, guys. This is amazing. Thank you."

In interviews David gave after the show he revealed that he had not expected to hear his name called. He could not have imagined that he would decisively beat the other David by earning 56 percent of the record-setting number of votes cast. Many viewers might also have thought that David Archuleta would win based on the praise heaped on the younger performer by the judges; Simon even predicted that David Archuleta would win *Idol*. He told the 17-year-old that he scored a knockout during

David is overcome with emotion as he is announced the winner during the *Idol* season seven finale. After a tearful moment, he immediately thanked his mother and brother for their support. David later said he was very surprised to win, and he praised the talent of runner-up David Archuleta.

the final competition with his version of "Imagine," a slow-paced, dreamy song written by the late Beatle John Lennon about living in a more perfect world.

DAVID ARCHULETA AND THE ARCHIES

The *American Idol* judges were correct when they said that both Davids were winners. David Archuleta, runner-up in season seven, has earned more than $1 million from album sales as well as ticket sales from his live concerts. His first single, "Crush," started out as number one on *Billboard* magazine's Hot 100 chart.

David James Archuleta was born on December 28, 1990, in Miami, Florida, and began entering and winning talent competitions at age 10. His family now lives in Murray, Utah, where David was mobbed by 10,000 people when he went back to visit his high school during the taping of *American Idol*.

David's important life influences include his Honduran-born mother and his American father, a jazz musician who was banned from *American Idol*'s rehearsal room because in his over-bearing manner he was interfering in his son's practice sessions.

Praised by the judges for his pure pop singing voice and admired by fans who call themselves "Archies," David's final three songs in the *Idol* competition were "Don't Let the Sun Go Down on Me," "In This Moment," and "Imagine." Winner David Cook said of his rival, "He has more talent at 17 than I know what to do with at 25."

Song Choice Criticized

Meanwhile, Simon found fault with the final song David Cook chose to sing in the competition. That song was "The World I Know," popularized by one of the older singer's favorite groups, Collective Soul. David accompanied himself on acoustic guitar. Simon said,

"I thought it was a beautiful song, but I'm going to be honest with you. It was completely and utterly the wrong song choice for you."

David (right) and David Archuleta share a duet during the season finale show. The two competitors had very different styles; David A. had a real pop singing voice, while David C. was more of a rock 'n' roller. In the end, David Cook's originality won the judges' favor.

Simon said David should have chosen one of the earlier songs he performed in the competition, such as the unique arrangement of the Michael Jackson hit "Billie Jean" or "Hello," a song by Lionel Richie.

Paula disagreed. She said, "I looked up at you on that stage and you're standing in your truth and you are delivering unbelievable songs with integrity and originality. And I truly applaud you, David Cook, I do."

Similarly, Randy praised him for having the courage to show different sides of himself with his music, including a sensitive side that contrasted with his usual rock 'n' roll side.

Apparently, Simon was troubled by his own words. After the final competition, he went home and watched performances by the two Davids again. This time he came away with a different conclusion: he no longer believed that David Archuleta's performance was the clear-cut favorite. And in a rare moment of self-reflection, during the results show Simon took back his earlier remarks, acknowledging that his comments to David had bordered on the disrespectful.

Surrounded by the other finalists, David sings "Time of My Life" during the *Idol* season finale. The song went on to be a hit single for the new Idol, who had been described as an "everydude." This meant that David's style had something to offer everyone and explained his popularity with fans.

"Everydude" Appeal

Clearly, the fans did not agree with Simon's earlier assessment of David's song choice when they selected him as the winner of *American Idol*. Perhaps they agreed with the assessment of MTV.com, which ranked David Cook as one of the 10 greatest *American Idol* contestants of all time. It said,

> **"With a voice tailor-made for modern-rock radio, an innate sense of humor and a penchant for taking risks with his arrangements, Cook was the 'everydude' who became king during the seventh season of *Idol*."**

The two Davids' final head-to-head competition had been billed as a boxing match with both coming out at one point wearing robes favored by boxers. But comparing the final matchup to a body contact sport did not sit well with David Cook, who decided to enjoy himself rather than go for blood. He was obviously having fun during one of his final performances when he sang with the iconic rock group ZZ Top, known for their long beards, sunglasses, and cool vibes, as they played "Sharp Dressed Man."

In the final moment of the results show, David performed his first duty as winner of *Idol*: singing "Time of My Life," which would be his first single. As he sang, the audience stood up and many people reached out to him. Confetti filled the air. "Time of My Life," which would go on to be a big hit for David, was written by Regie Hamm, winner of the *American Idol* Songwriter Contest. Hamm's upbeat song about weathering good times and bad received more than 500,000 online votes, more than any of the other 19 songs that made it to the final round. The song was an apt selection for David, who was also weathering some tough times in his life, notably the serious illness of his older half-brother. Still, David could not help reflecting that all of his hard work trying to make a name for himself in the music business had finally paid off.

David, a huge baseball fan, attends a game in a New York Yankees hat. He was an excellent pitcher in school, but his dreams for a sports career ended early. In addition to baseball, David has always been devoted to his music and his family.

2

Music, Baseball, and Brothers

David Cook grew up in a family that loved baseball. David, his parents, and two brothers often headed to Kauffman Stadium in Kansas City, Missouri, to watch the local baseball team, the Royals, play ball. The Cooks adopted the Royals as their team after they moved from Houston, Texas, about a year after David's birth on December 20, 1982.

The family relocated after a **hurricane** destroyed nearly everything they owned. They settled into the small town of Blue Springs near Kansas City. When David was 10, his father Stanley left the home after the family split up.

As David grew older, baseball was soon more than just a spectator sport for him. He was a talented pitcher in high school with a reliable fastball and dreams of turning professional after he graduated. Unfortunately, those dreams were shattered when a sports injury damaged his throwing arm. It was David's second major injury as a pitcher; the first was a **concussion** he received when he was hit in the head by a baseball.

Luckily for David, baseball was only one of his passions. Another was music. David first sang in public when he was in the fifth grade in a performance in which he had difficulty remembering the lyrics. Still, he was not discouraged. His grandmother recalled that David always enjoyed singing but did not like to listen to his recorded voice. She said that David was so bothered by the earliest tapes she recorded of him singing that he destroyed them.

First Guitar

David spent four years playing the violin, an instrument he took up mostly because a cute girl in the school orchestra also played it. When he was 12 his father gave him a Christmas present he would never forget: a Fender Stratocaster guitar, an instrument that David's father also played.

OUR LADY PEACE FAN

David loved the new guitar his father bought him for Christmas and learned to play it by imitating the styles of some of his favorite bands. One of those is a Canadian group called Our Lady Peace, which recorded a hit song titled "Clumsy" in 1997 when David was 15.

With members Raine Maida, Duncan Coutts, Jeremy Taggart, and Mike Turner, Our Lady Peace has produced seven albums and toured with Robert Plant of Led Zeppelin, Alanis Morissette, and Van Halen. The band has found success in Canada and the United States and is known for its hard-driving, alternative rock sound.

David is a big fan of Maida, the lead singer. During the *American Idol* competition, David sang one of Maida's best known songs, "Innocent." Later, David worked with Maida on the album he released after winning on *Idol*.

A visit to his grandmother's house in Indiana to hang out with his cousin turned into something much more. He recalled,

> **"One night we were having a slumber party, and Nine Inch Nails' 'Closer' came on the radio. I was like, 'That song is so cool.' There were a lot of changes going on at that point—I'd hit a growth spurt. I went to Indiana listening to country, and I came back listening to rock."**

Canadian band Our Lady Peace plays a street concert in Toronto. David has been a fan of the group since high school. He taught himself the guitar by listening to their albums and was excited to perform with lead singer Raine Maida during the *Idol* competition.

Such muscial groups as The Foo Fighters, Our Lady Peace, and Green Day caught his attention as well and he worked on his own guitar skills by playing along with their records. By the time he was 15 David had started a rock group called Axium with some friends.

Musical Theater

However, rock was not David's only musical interest. He also liked musical theater and in high school won lead roles in several musicals. He performed in *Singing in the Rain*, in which he also got to show off his comedy and gymnastics skills, as well as *The Music Man* and *West Side Story*. His theater teacher at Blue Springs South High School, Susan Cooper, recalled that even then David was capable of selling a song to an audience, a talent she described as rare among high school performers.

WEST SIDE STORY STAR

Whenever Blue Springs South High School put on a musical David could be counted on to win an important role. One of the roles David played was Riff in the musical *West Side Story*.

Originating as a Broadway play in 1957, *West Side Story* is a modern retelling of William Shakespeare's play *Romeo and Juliet*. Instead of the young lovers belonging to two feuding Italian families, in *West Side Story* the teens are separated by allegiances to two different gangs. Riff is the leader of the Jets, a group of white youths whose hated rivals are the Sharks, a gang of Puerto Rican kids. The title of the musical refers to the tough neighborhood on New York City's west side known as Hell's Kitchen.

The music for *West Side Story* was written by composer Leonard Bernstein and many of the songs are instantly recognizable by many generations. They include "Maria," "Somewhere," and "Tonight."

In 1961 *West Side Story* was made into a popular film that won 10 Academy Awards. It has been revived on Broadway several times, including a 2009 production. Its story of doomed love told with spirited singing and high-energy dancing makes it a favorite of high school performers.

The 1961 movie *West Side Story* is a tale of two teenagers from rival gangs who fall in love. David's talent won him several parts in musical theater during high school, including the character Riff in *West Side Story*. His teacher was impressed with David's ability to present a song to the audience.

In addition to baseball and theater, David was also active on the debate team. As a member of his high school's National Forensic League he won recognition for his communication and speaking skills. David also entered and won several talent competitions, including the Mr. Jaguar competition at Blue Springs South High, in which male high school students compete in formal wear and other categories.

Although he was bright, David admitted that he did not study hard and coasted through his high school classes. It was not until he was partially through college that he finally decided to get serious about studying. Before that he would skip classes if there was a conflict between playing in his band and studying.

DAViD COOK
ANALOG HEART

As a struggling musician David released his first CD, *Analog Heart,* in 2006. Marketing himself as a musician was a learning experience. And although it was sometimes difficult to make ends meet, David realized he wanted to make music his career.

Making His Own CD

Eventually David's high school band broke up and he decided to try a solo act. He made a demo CD of his songs, which he titled *Analog Heart*. He learned a lot from that experience. He said,

> **❝I'd never learned so much about myself as a musician than I did that year. I was struggling to book shows, struggling to get people to come to the shows, but I loved every second of it.❞**

At the age of 24, David graduated from Central Missouri State University with a degree in **graphic design.** Nevertheless he decided that his first love was still music. He decided to give himself until age 26 to make a living playing rock 'n' roll music. He left Missouri to live in Oklahoma, playing guitar with a band called Midwest Kings. To make ends meet he also worked as a bartender and house painter. Playing with the Midwest Kings gave David a lot of experience as a performer in ways he could not yet imagine.

One day David's younger brother Andrew told him that he planned to audition for *American Idol*. The boys' mother Beth planned to accompany Andrew. Would David like to join them in Nebraska for the audition? David, who would do anything for his brother, immediately agreed to go to support Andrew in his *Idol* audition.

Simon Fuller, the creator of *American Idol,* had a similar hit show in Britain. Although he had a hard time at first selling the idea to a U.S. network, *Idol* has gone on to create music superstars year after year. The show itself became a hit as well as a star-maker.

3

A Reliable Hit Machine

In Los Angeles several television executives cringe when *American Idol* is mentioned. For them, the show evokes memories of the unwise decisions they made when two Englishmen named Simon came to America with an idea for a music-based talent show competition they planned to call *American Idol.*

The two Simons—Simon Fuller and Simon Cowell—were convinced their reality show, which they launched in Britain under the name *Pop Idol*, was going to be a hit in Britain as well as America.

At the time, Simon Cowell was an executive with a British recording label. Simon Fuller was also a successful producer whose clients included the Spice Girls. In a profile on Fuller published in 2002, one newspaper wrote,

> ❝This shadowy 41-year-old . . . is the most significant figure in British pop music since Brian Epstein took the four young men who came into his Liverpool record store in 1961 and molded them into the Beatles.❞

Hard Sell

Under their concept, the program would show the harsh reality of auditioning. Selling their idea in England had been easy, and the two Simons believed that American television executives would also embrace its promise.

It didn't turn out that way; several network executives turned them down. Finally, the Fox network agreed to air the show in 2002. By then the British version, known as *Pop Idol*, was a hit with viewers who were becoming more than just fans because the outcome of the contest was determined by their votes. Said Simon Fuller,

> ❝Pure, simple television is not that interesting for me; what's far more interesting is trying to create a cult effect.❞

Kelly vs. Justin

Under the show's concept, contestants would try out in open auditions held in cities around the country. In the first season, 10,000 would-be pop stars between the ages of 16 and 24 auditioned with 10 selected as finalists.

The concept also called for a panel of celebrity judges to assess the talent and decide who would get the chance to compete. Joining the panel were Simon Cowell as well as record producer Randy Jackson and singer Paula Abdul.

The show premiered before an audience of 10 million. Three months later, with the competition whittled down to two finalists—Kelly Clarkson and Justin Guarini, more than 22 million people tuned in, using their votes to select Kelly as the first winner.

Kelly Clarkson, the first *Idol* winner, joins runner-up Justin Guarini during the season one finale. The show had premiered to an audience of 10 million; by the end of the season, the interactive nature of the show had caught fire with viewers, and audience numbers had more than doubled.

KELLY CLARKSON: *IDOL'S* FIRST WINNER

In early 2002, Kelly Clarkson was working as a cocktail waitress in Burleson, Texas. Nine months later, her name was a household word among America's pop music fans when she won the competition on the first season of *American Idol.* "Clarkson is everything you could ask for in a pop star and then some," said MTV.

Kelly has most certainly enjoyed an **incandescent** career, releasing four hit albums: *Thankful, Breakaway, My December,* and *All I Ever Wanted,* and she has won numerous awards including two Grammys.

Wild Card Winner

In season two, one of the stars who emerged was Ruben Studdard, a lovable 400-pound rhythm and blues, or R&B, singer from Birmingham, Alabama.

The other top contender was Clay Aiken, a skinny pop singer from North Carolina who hardly looked as though he could pass as a heartthrob. Nevertheless, the two unlikely competitors were clearly the most talented singers in the field.

Clay had been voted off the show but was brought back in the Wild Card round—a second chance built into the rules that gives contestants an opportunity to return. Still, when Clay went head-to-head against Ruben, the "velvet teddy bear," he fell short, albeit by just 134,000 votes out of the 24 million cast in the season finale.

Public Outcry

Clay may have lost, but in the years following the end of season two he has sold more albums than Ruben, a trend that other runners-up on *Idol* would continue. In season three, Jennifer Hudson finished well back in the pack but went on to win an Academy Award for her role in the film *Dreamgirls* as well as a Grammy for her first album.

The title in season three was won by Fantasia Barrino, a 19-year-old with a background as a **gospel music** singer. In the finals, in which 65 million fans voted, Fantasia edged out 16-year-old Diana DeGarmo. Said Simon Cowell,

> **❝America got it 100 percent right. There aren't many other artists in America right now that I'd prefer to have on my label.❞**

Changing the Rules

Season four premiered under new rules that raised the age limit to 28. That enabled 28-year-old rocker Bo Bice to enter the competition. Bo would last until the final week, facing country singer Carrie Underwood.

Simon predicted Carrie would win but Bo had his backers as well, including guest judge Clive Davis, the powerful RCA Records head. After Bo performed the Elton John hit, "Don't Let the Sun Go Down On Me," Davis said, "Bo, you really captured the tone. It was heartfelt. It was powerful. It was passionate."

Still, the fans responded to Carrie's immense talent and made her the winner. Carrie has not let down her fans; she has released two hit albums, establishing herself as one of the top stars in country music.

Season four runner-up Bo Bice and winner Carrie Underwood perform a duet during the *Idol* finale. That year the age limit was raised, which allowed Bo to compete. His powerful style was a hit with fans and judges alike, but in the end Carrie's talent won her the crown.

Ironic End

Season five featured something for nearly everyone: pop singers Katharine McPhee and Taylor Hicks, R&B singer Elliott Yamin, country singer Kellie Pickler, and rocker Chris Daughtry. Each competitor received tremendous audience support, but as the weeks wore on they started falling out of contention.

Kellie was voted off April 26. Chris left on May 10—his departure was a shock because the press picked Chris to win. Elliott was a fan favorite because he had overcome adversity to make it as far as he had—he was a high school dropout and diabetic.

Season six top 3 finalists (from left) Melinda Doolittle, Blake Lewis, and Jordin Sparks share the *Idol* stage. Melinda was voted off in third place. Jordin edged out Blake and became the show's youngest winner at age 17.

But Elliott left on May 17, leaving Taylor and Katharine alone in the finale, which was won by Taylor. Ironically, Taylor and Katharine have been able to put together only modest careers while Elliott, Chris, and Kellie have released hit albums.

ROCKING ON *IDOL*

David Cook could not have picked a better role model than Chris Daughtry. Chris finished fourth on season five but the hard-rocker from North Carolina was offered the chance to be lead singer of one of his favorite groups, Fuel. He declined, instead electing to front his own band.

It was a wise decision. His band, Daughtry, has produced an album that has remained at the top of the charts for two years. The album, *Daughtry*, has sold more than 5 million copies.

Youngest Winner

In season six, the stage first belonged to Sanjaya Malakar, a shy teenager who emerged as a fan favorite even though the judges questioned his talent.

Another fan favorite was R&B singer Melinda Doolittle. When Melinda sang the jazz standard, "My Funny Valentine," Simon responded, "That was incredible. To me, without question, it is the best vocal we've had in the competition."

But neither Sanjaya nor Melinda would be around for the finale. Instead, the finalists were Blake Lewis, a strong performer able to sing rock, R&B, country, and music in other **genres**, and Jordin Sparks, a pop and R&B singer. In the final few weeks Jordin gave stirring performances of hits by such stars as Barbra Streisand, Donna Summer, and Christina Aguilera. Jordin is the youngest competitor to ever win on *American Idol*; at just 17 when she won, Jordin has many years to duplicate the success of the stars with whom she has been compared.

David's guitar displays the letters AC in honor of his brothers Adam and Andrew. David originally went to *Idol* tryouts in Nebraska just to support Andrew, who then talked David into auditioning. Both were shocked when David unexpectedly won an invitation to the next round of the competition.

4

Unexpected Winner

Many brothers are close, but not too many would do what David did for his younger brother Andrew. Not only did David fly to Omaha, Nebraska, to be with Andrew when he tried out for *American Idol* in August 2007, but he also stood in the rain with him at 5:30 A.M. waiting for admission to the Omaha Qwest Center.

Getting up before the sun rose and getting a little wet did not faze David, who was merely there to support his brother. But Andrew also talked him into trying out for the show. Andrew's audition did not go well but David's did. David was as surprised as anyone because he never pictured *American Idol* as a path to his own success.

Cameras captured David's first performance in front of Randy, Paula, and Simon; David sang "Livin' On a Prayer," a rock song originally performed by Bon Jovi. With a **soul patch** beneath his lip and his brown hair fixed in a **faux-hawk**, David told the judges he thought he had what it takes to be the next *American Idol* because "I bring something a little bit different to the table." The night before his audition he watched season five competitor Chris Daughtry's performances to observe what Chris had done that had made him successful. David concluded about his own prospects:

> **"I think my voice is strong enough to carry me through. It's just a question of whether or not I have what they are looking for."**

Going to Hollywood

David's initial performance received promising feedback from the judges. The only criticism came from Randy, who thought David needed to display more emotion.

As soon as David heard that he was going on in the competition, he gave his mother a big hug, lifting her off the ground.

David was one of 164 *American Idol* hopefuls invited to Hollywood, and he eventually became one of the top 12 finalists, along with David Archuleta. The others were Syesha Mercado, Jason Castro, Brooke White, Carly Smithson, Kristy Lee Cook, Ramiele Malubay, Michael Johns, Chikezie, Amanda Overmyer, and David Hernandez.

On the program David benefited from his unique life experiences. Through high school and college he played with two bands whose regular gigs gave him plenty of face time in front of audiences. He already self-produced a CD. And his high school musical appearances taught him how to get in character to sing a particular song and how to make the whole process of singing look effortless. One reporter had this to say about David:

> **"Cook gets it. He played the swaggering, sexy dude with his covers of Free's 'All Right**

Now' and the Beatles' 'Day Tripper,' then soft-ened up as the wounded yet gracious ex-lover [for Mariah Carey's 'Always Be My Baby'] and the swoony swain [Lionel Richie's 'Hello']. **"**

Unusual Arrangements

David also knew how to make the most of his **tenor** voice by selecting unusual arrangements of the songs he chose. He was applauded by the judges for his willingness to take risks and show his vocal range. When he sang a 1960s song called "Happy

David performs The Beatles' song "Eleanor Rigby" during the top 12 competition. Early on he impressed the judges with his self-confidence, unique style, and unusual arrangements of the songs he chose. The usually critical Simon even commented that David could go on to win the *Idol* title.

Together," by the group The Turtles, Randy said it was "crazy." And Simon allowed, "If he can pull this off, he can do anything." Simon went even further after David sang The Beatles' "Eleanor Rigby," during the show dedicated to the songwriting team of Beatles John Lennon and Paul McCartney. Simon said,

> **❝If this show remains a talent competition rather than a popularity competition, you actually could win this entire show.❞**

David impressed the judges again when the contestants were asked to choose a song from the year they were born. He chose "Billie Jean," which had been a smash for Michael Jackson in 1982.

Idol season seven top 5 finalists pose with mentor Neil Diamond (third from right). Although the young hopefuls learned a lot from such famous artists, fewer guest coaches appeared that season because the producers felt they took too much of the spotlight away from the show's contestants.

But the arrangement David chose for the song, which he borrowed from musician Chris Cornell, turned it into a completely different song from what the public expected. Michael's version was a bouncy pop song; David performed "Billie Jean" as a slow ballad. The risk paid off with all three judges loving it.

David was also widely praised the week that country singer Dolly Parton appeared on the show. He sang Dolly's "Little Sparrow," which prompted Randy to say, "You're a rocker, but I like how you've been showing you've got this unbelievable range. You made your own arrangement which was very cool. And once again another hot, consistent performance."

LEARNING FROM THE BEST

Mariah Carey and Dolly Parton were not the only guest coaches to work with contestants during season seven. Other musical stars who added their celebrity to the *Idol* season included Andrew Lloyd Webber, a Grammy, Tony, and Academy Award–winning composer of such musicals as *Cats* and *Phantom of the Opera*, and singer-songwriter Neil Diamond, whose 40-year musical career has spawned such hit songs as "Sweet Caroline," "Cherry, Cherry," and "Song Sung Blue." Diamond is a member of the Songwriters Hall of Fame and a recipient of its lifetime achievement award.

Overall, fewer celebrity mentors were present for season seven than season six. The show's producers felt that too many mentors took time away from their ability to showcase the show's contestants.

Health Concerns

Later that night David received some unwelcome attention when he became ill. David has **high blood pressure**, which is normally well controlled by medication but can be aggravated by stress. David was taken to the hospital for observation and then released. His sudden hospitalization made news.

Another stressful part of David's life was coping with the serious illness of his older half-brother, Adam, a married man with children, who suffered from brain cancer. The cancer had been inactive for many years but returned in 2006. Adam was undergoing **chemotherapy** during the time David was on *Idol*. Adam was able to make it to one performance. He was in the audience during the week that singer and songwriter Mariah Carey was a guest coach on the program, and David put a rock spin on her hit, "Always Be My Baby."

Mariah commented that David's song choice was not a natural one for a male singer, and she felt proud as a songwriter to know that the song worked from a male perspective. Randy, Paula, and Simon were equally blown away by David's performance. Simon said,

> **❝It was like coming out of karaoke hell into a breath of fresh air. That was original, it was daring, it stood out by a mile. This is the sign of a great potential artist—someone who takes risks.❞**

Helping Kids

Mariah was one of many stars who also appeared on the special Idol Gives Back charity concert on April 9, 2008. Also appearing on the program were actor-comedian Robin Williams, comedian Dane Cook, football player Peyton Manning, and actor Kiefer Sutherland. *Idol* alumni Elliott Yamin, Fantasia, Chris Daughtry,

IDOL GIVES BACK

The Idol Gives Back charity event in which David took part was the second event under the program; both raised about $75 million that was donated to six charities. Donations were made by celebrities and corporations, and viewers were encouraged to phone in pledges during the program or to pledge money through a Web site.

Charities that benefit from Idol Gives Back are the Children's Defense Fund, The Global Fund, Make It Right, Malaria No More, Save the Children, U.S. Fund for UNICEF, and the Children's Health Fund.

David appears with other finalists at the 2008 Idol Gives Back concert. Singers, comedians, actors, and *Idol* alumni all appeared at the second annual charity event. Their talent and desire to help others shone that night as they raised money to benefit children all over the world.

and Carrie Underwood were also joined by singers Miley Cyrus, Bono, Snoop Dogg, John Legend, and Gloria Estefan, and the groups Maroon 5 and Heart.

The final eight contestants, including David, also sang several songs as a group including "Shout to the Lord," "Seasons of Love" from the play *Rent*, and "Please Don't Stop the Music," a Rihanna song.

As always, the seventh season had its share of drama, which led to some unexpected downfalls. One of them occurred during a week devoted to songs by composer Andrew Lloyd Webber when Brooke forgot the words to the song, "You Must Love Me." For the first time ever on the program, she stopped mid-song and began again. That same night, Jason was criticized for singing "Memory," a well-known song from the Broadway show *Cats* almost always performed by older female singers.

Neither Jason nor Brooke ended up being voted off the show, most likely because viewers felt sympathy for them. Instead Carly, who sang "Superstar," the title song from the Webber play *Jesus Christ Superstar*, in a nearly flawless performance, was voted out, probably because viewers figured she would be safe and cast their votes for others.

David thanks judges Paula, Simon, and Randy during the season finale. Both Davids performed well in the finale, and the suspense built until the very last moment. When David Cook won, Simon said he would be known as one of *Idol's* greatest talents.

Some Surprises

Jason also figured in another startling moment that took place on April 29, when only five contestants were left. Paula commented on a song that Jason had not even sung, raising suspicions that the program followed a script.

Another surprise was the elimination of Michael, a handsome Australian singer who had never been in the bottom three. Nevertheless, he was voted off after he sang "Dream On," which was popularized by Aerosmith. Boos could be heard when his elimination was announced, leaving seven contestants.

Few people were surprised when Syesha was voted off the program on May 14. That left only the two popular Davids in the competition. Both were likable, both had never been in the bottom three, and both had huge fan bases. Not surprisingly David Archuleta's base was tween girls; David Cook's fans were older with a substantial number of them falling into the middle age range.

Down to the Wire

During the season finale David Archuleta could not hide his nervousness. David Cook was calm. Each sang three songs. David Cook performed the U2 song "I Still Haven't Found What I'm Looking For," Collective Soul's "The World I Know," and Emily Shackelton's "Dream Big."

David Archuleta turned in strong performances on his three final songs. But when the votes were tallied David Cook posted a significant victory, and one that was foreseen by Simon Fuller. He said,

"I wasn't surprised Cook won, but that's because I get to see all the results each week. I don't want to tempt fate, but I think David's name will enter the list of great talents discovered by *Idol*."

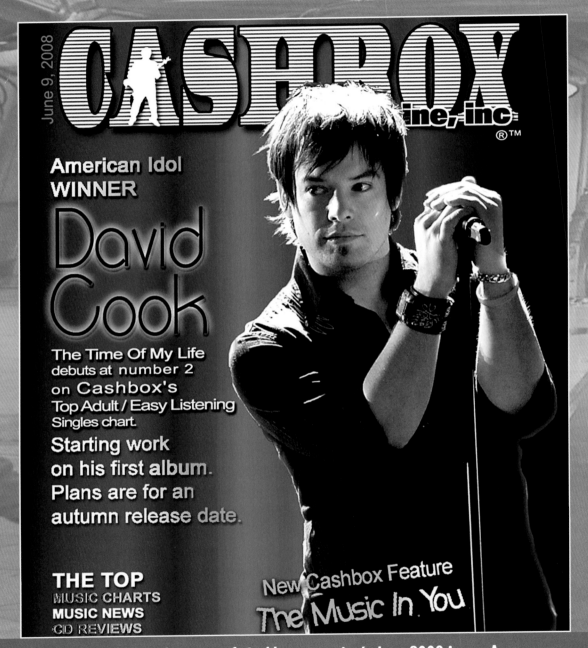

June 9, 2008

CASHBOX
ine, inc ®™

American Idol WINNER

David Cook

The Time Of My Life debuts at number 2 on Cashbox's Top Adult / Easy Listening Singles chart.

Starting work on his first album. Plans are for an autumn release date.

THE TOP
MUSIC CHARTS
MUSIC NEWS
CD REVIEWS

New Cashbox Feature
The Music In You

David is featured on the cover of *Cashbox* magazine's June 2008 issue. As soon as he won the *Idol* crown, he became an instant celebrity. His music quickly appeared everywhere, too, and he soon had a record 11 songs on the *Billboard* Hot 100 chart.

5

Instant Celebrity

Big things started happening for David after he was crowned winner on *American Idol*. Songs he performed on the show began selling as MP3 downloads, quickly giving him 11 songs on *Billboard* magazine's Hot 100 chart. No individual artist or group had been able to do that since 1964 when The Beatles placed 14 songs on the Hot 100.

Among those songs were "The Time of My Life," "I Still Haven't Found What I'm Looking For," "Hello," and "The World I Know."

David's desire to be an important name in the music business was coming true more quickly than he had imagined. Nevertheless, he took the leap forward in his characteristically modest way. He said,

> **You want to talk about humbling. To be in the same sentence, or even the same paragraph, as the Beatles is . . . I can't really put together an intelligent response other than to say, 'Wow.'**

Dating a Former *Idol* Contestant

In fact, David's life had already taken a rapid turn the evening of the results show. Before he entered the Nokia Theater, David was interviewed by Justin Guarini, season one runner-up, and Kimberly Caldwell, a season two semifinalist. Justin and Kimberly were working as hosts for the TV show *Idol Tonight*. As the interview progressed David said to Kimberly,

> **I'm just excited because I finally get to talk to you. I've been hearing you say all these nice things about me all season, so I'm actually going to ask you to dinner right now.**

Out of the blue, David had impulsively asked Kimberly for a date while the cameras were rolling. Later, after thinking it over, he regretted asking her out so publicly. Fortunately the pretty Kimberly said yes and she and David hugged. The two dated for about eight months before amicably parting.

Successful *Idol* Tour

With a busy schedule David did not have a lot of time to devote to dating, anyway. His first priority was performing with the other nine semifinalists in the *American Idol* arena tour. That summer he sang in more than 50 cities across America, starting in Arizona in July and ending in September in Tulsa, Oklahoma, the city in which he had been working before *Idol*.

David strolls with his girlfriend Kimberly Caldwell, a semifinalist on *Idol* season two who interviewed David the night he won. The two went out for a while in 2008, but David's busy schedule didn't leave him much room for dating, and they soon parted as friends.

David reveled in the opportunity to spend more time with some of his friends from the show. They included Mike Johns, Archie, Luke Menard, and Amy Davis. And he was happy to be appearing in front of smaller audiences than *Idol* attracted and not to have to worry about whether his performances were good enough to ensure that he would make it to the next round. The tour was a big success; nearly a half-million fans came to the shows, bringing in nearly $30 million in proceeds, nearly $9 million more than the 2006 *Idol* tour.

One of the fun things David and his fellow *Idol* tour partici-
pants got to do was to ring the closing bell on the **NASDAQ**
exchange in August when the tour was in New York City. Serving
as a spokesperson for all the performers, David took the time to
thank all the sponsors for the tour, including Kellogg's Pop Tarts
and Guitar Hero, and to mention that CKX, the parent company
of 19 Entertainment, which runs the *Idol* franchise, is one of the
companies whose shares are traded on the NASDAQ.

David was proud of his self-titled CD, which came out in 2008. He was thrilled
to work on the album with many of his musical heroes. Although not all critics
praised his efforts, the album went on to sell more than a million copies.

Proud of the Record

Touring was demanding but David also had another big concern on his mind: planning his first post-*Idol* record album. His goal was to bring out his first album in early November, which gave him only three months to write and record it.

David was working with some talented people he greatly respected, but because he was on the road he had to do a lot of the work with them through emails and telephone calls. Working with David on the project were Green Day producer Rob Cavallo, the Goo-Goo Dolls' Johnny Rzeznik, Our Lady Peace's Raine Maida, and Audioslave's Chris Cornell.

David, who co-wrote most of the songs on his self-titled album, *David Cook*, that debuted on November 18, 2008, always knew what kind of record he wanted to make. He said,

> **I'm not trying to surprise people now: I'm putting out a rock record. I just want the songs to kick you in the teeth or make you want to cry—or do something drastic, like jump off a building. I want somebody to be exhausted when they're done listening.**

Making an album that reflected who David was in such a short period of time was no easy feat, and David was especially grateful to be working with so many of his musical heroes. He described this collaborative arrangement as not unlike "going to Disneyland everyday." David also said,

> **To work with these people that I've looked up to for years and have them treat me as a peer was the most fun aspect of this whole process. I remember my first writing session was with Raine [Maida] from Our Lady Peace?—like my favorite band, my favorite singer. I was so nervous, 'cause you always**

worry about these people that you put on this pedestal, are they going to be jerks, you know? And Raine was the exact opposite— I mean just so chill, so extremely gracious. **"**

Record Reviews

Music journalist Don Waller, who reviewed the album, said David's vocals "sound good, strong and totally professional, with the distinctive character and sandpapery timbre that are instantly familiar to those who watched the show." But he was not so enthusiastic about the album cut "Light On." He faulted it for its "by-the-numbers generic power balladry, a song that could be anybody from Green Day to My Chemical Romance." Added a reviewer for *USA Today*:

"You'll search in vain for a spark of originality, but you will find a degree of poignancy in songs about Cook's cancer-stricken brother, Adam ["A Daily AntheM," whose capitalized letters spell out his name, and especially "Permanent," a moving semi-ballad]. Still, you have to hope there's more to Cook than is audible in this disappointing debut. **"**

Nonetheless, *David Cook* was a huge success as was "Light On," the first single which debuted at number 17 on the Hot 100. Meanwhile, its video was watched more than a million times the day it was featured on AOL's PopEater blog. The album went on to be certified platinum, meaning it sold more than a million copies, and was a large factor in helping David to earn $2 million by that summer.

As David's celebrity grew companies began flooding him with offers to linking their products to his name. The sneaker company Skechers USA quickly signed him to help promote their athletic shoes. The company now has the right to use his image in its worldwide advertisements. Celebrity endorsement deals like David got from Skechers can make stars a lot of money.

TV Star

Also coming David's way were opportunities to appear on television programs. Even before he cut his album he won the Teen Choice Award for Male Reality Star in 2008. Along with David Archuleta he also served as a presenter on the show. The two singers presented an award to Miley Cyrus. David also found himself as a guest on *TRL*'s Spanish version, *Live With Regis & Kelly*, as well as *The View*.

Having a high profile did not change David's view of himself. He said,

> **When people look at me as a rock star, it seems humorous to me. I look at myself as a goober.**

David performs on *Saturday Night Live,* one of many TV appearances he made after winning the *Idol* title. He felt nervous about the *SNL* show because so many other famous musicians had appeared on that stage. Nevertheless, millions of fans loved his performance that night.

David plays and sings on *The View*. After *Idol*, he appeared on daytime talk shows, the Teen Choice Awards, and the pages of *People* magazine. He was becoming a big name, but David was the same down-to-earth guy as before. He kept his sense of humor throughout all the new publicity.

GUEST STAR ON *SNL*

David was nervous when he was slated to appear on *Saturday Night Live*, which for more than three decades has been host to many famous musical acts. The musical guest the week before David's appearance was Coldplay, while Beyoncé followed him the week after. Other *American Idol* alumni who have appeared on the popular late night program include Clay Aiken, Carrie Underwood, and Kelly Clarkson.

David appeared on the November 1, 2008 program, which was watched by more than 12 million viewers. David explained why he was so worried: "Dress rehearsal was full of nausea and dry heaves. It was so nerve-racking because it was our big unveiling as a band. I listened to the performances [of "Light On" and "Declaration"] the day after, and you can hear some timidness in my voice."

David talked about his win with talk show host Ellen DeGeneres on her program and sang "The World I Know" for her audience. He also confided to Ellen that his ambitions include winning Oscar, Grammy, and Tony awards.

David and David Archuleta made a joint appearance on *The View* when the show made a visit to Las Vegas, Nevada, in June. Filmed outdoors, David sang "Time of My Life" during the appearance with his mother and Archie's father in the audience.

David was also honored as one of 2008's hottest bachelors by *People* magazine, which asked him a series of questions on what he looks for in a woman (someone with compassion and confidence); whether he would date a fan (he would not rule it out); and where he expected to be in five years. He replied,

"I see myself being happy doing whatever I'm doing, whether it's continuing to play shows all over the country or working at a gas station. I have no idea. Anything can happen."

David joins Minnie Mouse during the grand opening of the American Idol Experience at Disney World in Florida. After *Idol*, he was having the time of his life, attending special events, touring, and performing for Senator Hillary Clinton and American troops in the Middle East.

6

The Time of His Life

As 2008 came to a close, David found the opportunity to sing before one of his biggest fans—Hillary Clinton. The United States senator from New York and former first lady had earlier that year conducted a historic but ill-fated campaign to be the Democratic Party's first female nominee for president.

Senator Clinton, who would later be appointed secretary of state by President Obama, had publicly revealed that she voted for David in the *Idol* competition and that her favorite song from the show was David's version of Roberta Flack's "The First Time Ever I Saw Your Face." The song had been Simon's choice for David during the show's finale.

David was honored to sing for Hillary in Carnegie Hall in New York City, one of the premiere performance halls in the country, as part of *Glamour* magazine's Woman of the Year Awards. Hillary was one of the women honored at the ceremony for inspiring women with her historic run for the presidency.

College Tour

As 2009 dawned David continued his momentum by appearing on *Good Morning America* to announce his college tour—mtvU Presents David Cook's Declaration Tour, which would kick off in

David joins hosts Diane Sawyer and Steve Gilbert on *Good Morning America* to announce his upcoming Declaration tour. David was excited to bring back the old-fashioned kind of college tour, in which he and his band would promote their music in cities across the country.

mid-February. David and his band were slated to visit college towns across America. The 50-city tour was planned as old-fashioned homage to the way bands used to promote their music. David described his excitement over the tour:

"There's something inherently nostalgic about playing college shows. So many amazing acts used to do it, so it's nice to be able to bring that ideal back, in some small way. And besides, touring on a bus beats what we used to do, which was cram five guys into a seven-passenger van for one show, 13 hours away."

The *Good Morning America* segment was taped in Florida to coincide with the opening of the new American Idol Experience attraction at Disney's Hollywood Studios theme park, which David helped to launch with a concert.

SEVEN *IDOL* WINNERS, ONE STAGE

In February 2009, David Cook was one of seven *American Idol* winners who were on hand for the opening of a new attraction at Disney's Hollywood Studios theme park in Buena Vista, Florida. They were there to launch the American Idol Experience, which gives ordinary people a chance to experience what it might be like to actually audition and perform on an exact replica of the *Idol* set.

People "audition" at the attraction in front of judges who resemble the actual television show personalities while the audience decides whether the audition was good enough to merit a real tryout on the show. If the audience approves, the contestant will get a pass to go to the head of the line at the next real *American Idol* audition.

Sharing the stage with David at the opening were *Idol* winners Jordin Sparks, Taylor Hicks, Carrie Underwood, Fantasia Barrino, Ruben Studdard, and Kelly Clarkson. Host Ryan Seacrest, judge Paula Abdul and former contestants David Archuleta, Ace Young, Jason Castro, Mandisa, LaKisha Jones, Phil Stacey, Carly Smithson, and Michael Johns were also present. David performed "Light On" and a duet with Carrie.

David seems poised and ready to be in the spotlight for years to come. He has said his ambitions include winning Oscar, Grammy, and Tony awards. But wherever his musical path leads, he will always remember his start on *American Idol* and the many fans who have helped him reach for his dreams.

Saying Thank You

Ever mindful of the role his fans have been playing in his success, David made sure to update them frequently on his Web site with video blog segments. The Web site, which was maintained by David's label, Sony BMG, crashed on the first day when so many eager fans tried to access it.

Wanting to say thank you to American soldiers serving in Iraq and Kuwait, David also completed a tour sponsored by United Service Organizations, also known as the USO. David performed at seven bases, where he signed autographs for many of the soldiers.

David also helped raise money to fund research for brain cancer, the malady that afflicted his older brother Adam for a decade. In May David lost his brother to that disease, but the next day David appeared at the 12th annual Race for Hope 5K event in Washington, D.C., where he not only joined the race but was honorary chairman. He said that his brother would have wanted him to be there. David's team raised nearly $100,000 for cancer research.

David spent his first year as the winner of *American Idol* in a whirlwind of activity, but he also found himself back on the *Idol* stage at the Nokia Theater. During the 2009 *Idol* season he performed "Permanent," a song from his first album. All proceeds from the live version of the song, which was available for purchase as an MP3 download, were earmarked for Accelerate Brain Cancer Cure, a Washington, D.C., organization David supports whose mission is to find better treatments and a cure for brain cancer.

Relaxing at Home

When David finds the time to relax he likes to spend time with his family, including his younger brother Andrew, who has teased his big brother by placing his own high school "best vocalist" trophy next to David's platinum album plaque.

David always thinks about both of his brothers when he plays his guitars, which bear the initials AC in their honor. He'd like to get married and have his own family one day.

What's ahead for David? Perhaps he will win a Grammy or an Oscar as some of his fellow *Idol* alumni have already done. Certainly there will be other rock albums and collaborations with musicians he admires. He will continue to push himself to be the best he can be and will remain thankful for the opportunity he got through his "accidental" victory on *American Idol*.

1982 David Roland Cook born on December 20, 1982, in Houston, Texas.

1983 Family moves to Missouri after Hurricane Alicia destroys their home.

1994 Father buys David his first guitar.

1997 Starts band called Axium.

2000 Graduates from Blue Springs South High School.

2006 Graduates from Central Missouri State University with a degree in graphic design.

Moves to Tulsa, Oklahoma, and joins a band called Midwest Kings.

Releases *Analog Heart*.

2007 Enters *American Idol* competition.

2008 After months of competing against other singers, wins the seventh *American Idol* competition on May 21.

Meets and begins dating Kimberly Caldwell, *Idol* season two finalist in May.

First single, "Light On," released.

Breaks *Billboard* record with 11 songs on the Hot 100 list in a single week.

Releases the album *David Cook* in November.

Relationship with Kimberly Caldwell ends in December.

2009 *David Cook* certified platinum.

Declaration Tour visits college towns starting in February.

Attends the grand opening of Disney's American Idol Experience at Disney World in February.

Brother Adam dies of brain cancer in May.

Together with David Archuleta holds a concert in Manila, Philippines, on May 16.

Returns to the *American Idol* stage during season eight finale to perform his song "Permanent" in honor of his late brother Adam.

Awards, Nominations, and Honors

2006   *Analog Heart* wins *Urban Tulsa Weekly*'s Indie Album of the Year Award.

2008   Wins *American Idol*.

Wins Teen Choice Male Reality Star award.

Wins The New Music Awards Top 40 Male Artist of the Year.

Named one of 2008's Hottest Bachelors by *People* magazine.

Sings for former First Lady Hillary Clinton.

2009   Album certified platinum.

Nominated for Teen Choice awards for Breakout Artist and Album (Male Artist).

Singles

2008   "Light On"

2009   "Come Back to Me"
"Permanent"

Albums

2006   *Analog Heart*

2008   *David Cook*

Music Videos

2008   "Light On"

2009   "Come Back to Me"

concussion—Brain injury that often occurs during sports from a blow to the head or a fall; symptoms include headaches and confusion.

chemotherapy—Chemical mixture that attacks cancer cells but can also damage healthy cells.

faux-hawk—Hairstyle related to the mohawk but does not involve shaving the head.

genres—Category of pieces of music that share a certain style or theme; for example, rhythm and blues or rock.

gospel music—Spiritual music often sung in African-American churches, a forerunner to soul music or rhythm and blues.

graphic design—Art of using visual elements such as type faces, line drawings, and photographs to create appealing advertisements, logos, and Web pages.

high blood pressure—Silent but dangerous medical condition in which blood pumped from the heart under too great pressure damages arteries and veins; untreated, it can lead to heart attack and stroke.

hurricane—Massive storm characterized by winds over 75 miles per hour and heavy rains that can produce flooding and other damage.

incandescent—Shining or brilliant.

NASDAQ—National Association of Securities Dealers Automated Quotations, a stock exchange where shares of companies are bought and sold by investors.

soul patch—Well-trimmed facial hair under the lip once favored by jazz musicians.

tenor—Male voice in the middle range, falling in between alto and bass.

Books and Periodicals

Berson, Misha. "Finalist David Cook's Theater Chops Set the Stage for 'Idol' Success." *The Seattle Times* (March 17, 2008): http://seattletimes.nwsource.com/html/television/2004419958_davidcook17.html.

Cowell, Simon. *I Don't Mean to Be Rude, But . . . : Backstage Gossip from American Idol & the Secrets that Can Make You a Star.* New York: Broadway Books, 2003.

Gundersen, Edna. "Introducing 'David Cook'; Fans Know the Rocker from *American Idol,* But Today's Release Defines Him, He Says." *USA Today* (November 18, 2008): p. D-1.

Holden, Stephen. "*Idol* Finale: (Pop) Power to the People." *New York Times* (May 23, 2008): http://movies.nytimes.com/2008/05/23/arts/television/23idol.html.

Lang, Derrick J. "How David Cook Won *American Idol.*" *Pittsburgh Post-Gazette* (May 23, 2008): p. E3.

Menze, Jill. "Cook-ing With Gas." *Billboard* (November 15, 2008): p. 37.

Scaggs, Austin. "America's Accidental Idol." *Rolling Stone* (June 26, 2008): p. 29-30.

Web Sites

www.abc2.org

The Web site for the Accelerate Brain Cancer Cure Foundation, a Washington, D.C.-based group supported by David Cook that hopes to accelerate a cure for brain cancer. The site includes a link to download David's song, "Permanent," and discusses the organization's mission.

www.americanidol.com

American Idol's official Web site includes information on the current season's contestants, including episode recaps, a map showing where the contestants live, and information about *American Idol*'s charity, Idol Gives Back.

www.davidcookofficial.com

The official Web site for David Cook includes information on his media appearances, fan forums, and a video blog from the artist himself.

www.nflonline.org

This is the official Web site for the National Forensic League, the organization that hosts national debating competitions like the ones in which David Cook participated while in high school.

ABOUT THE AUTHOR

Gail Snyder is a freelance writer and advertising copywriter who has written more than 15 books for young readers. She lives in Chalfont, Pennsylvania, with her husband Hal, and daughter Ashley.